Moving into English

Authors

Alma Flor Ada • F. Isabel Campoy • Yolanda N. Padrón • Nancy Roser

Harcourt

Orlando   Austin   Chicago   New York   Toronto   London   San Diego

Visit *The Learning Site!*
www.harcourtschool.com

ISBN 0-15-334271-4

12 13 14 15 030 12 11 10 09

Contents

Hello, _____

To the Teacher
Help children trace the word *Hello* and write their name on the line. Then ask them to draw a picture of themselves similar to the cover of *Literature Big Book: Hello, Lulu.*

Lesson 1: Words of the Week

Name _____

Lesson 1: Respond to Literature

To the Teacher
Ask children to point to and name the people and things that are important to Lulu on the left. Then have them draw their own family and things in the empty house. Help children compare their own family, friends, and interests to those of Lulu.

Name _____

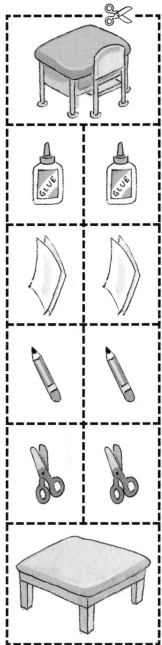

To the Teacher
Have children cut out the small pictures of classroom items. Tell children to glue
each cutout in an appropriate place in the classroom.

Lesson 2: Words of the Week

To the Teacher
Have children draw things they use at school on the desk.

Name _____

To the Teacher

Have children cut out the people. Then have them match each cutout with the appropriate family member in the picture as you say each family word: *mother, father, sister, brother, grandmother,* and *grandfather.*

Lesson 3: Words of the Week

Name_____

To the Teacher
Help children identify small Willa and big Willa. Have them draw lines matching small Willa to things she likes and does now. Then have them draw lines from big Willa to the things she will do by herself when she is big.

Lesson 3: Respond to Literature

Name _____

To the Teacher
Have children circle each part of the body as you name it: *head, eyes, nose, ears, mouth, hands, arms, legs, feet,* and *body.*

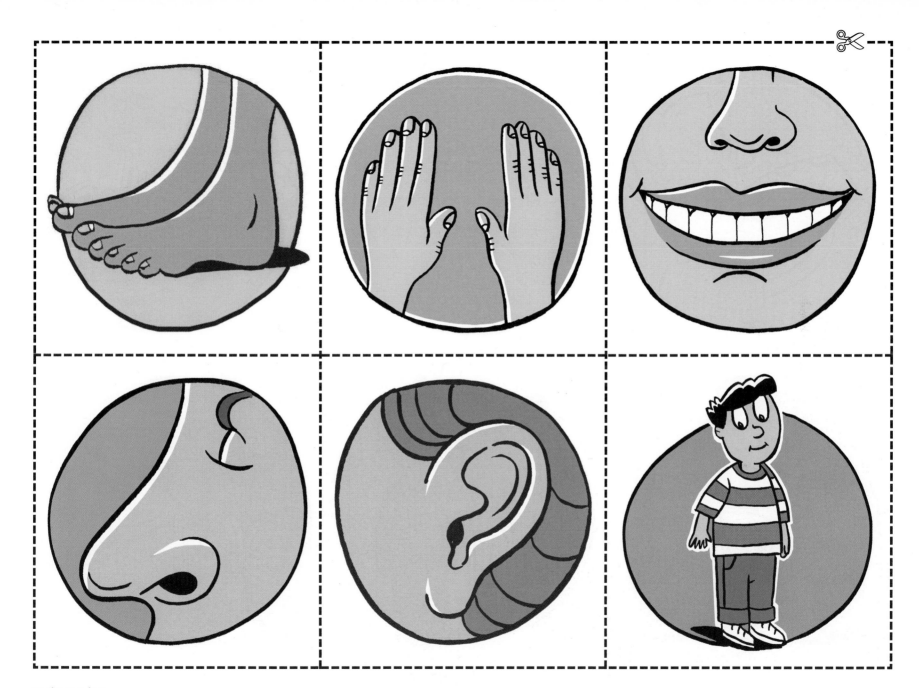

To the Teacher

Help children cut apart the cards and place them on a desk with the body part face up. Have partners take turns picking a card, naming the body part, and recalling how that part was used in *The Body Book*. Then have them turn the card over to see if they were correct.

Lesson 4: Respond to Literature

 my pal

8

My Pal

by Kenneth Choi   illustrated by Michelle Berg

Harcourt

Unit 1: Take-Home Book

my cap

my bus

7

18

6

my bag

my pen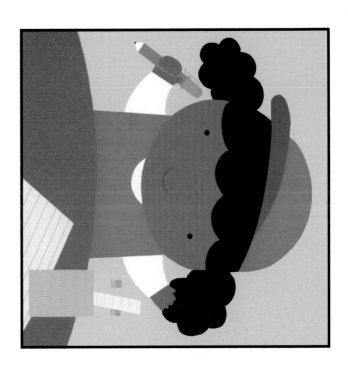

3

19

Unit 1: Take-Home Book

my box

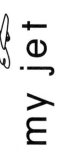

my jet

4

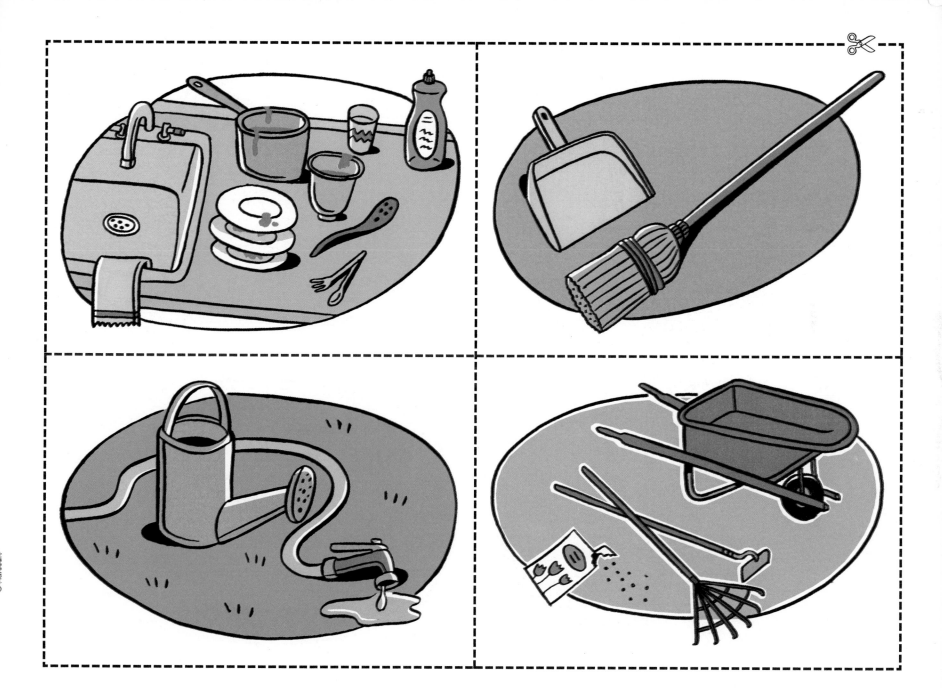

To the Teacher
Have partners discuss how they would use the items pictured on each card. Then
have them cut out the cards, turn them over, and tell a story about how the wolves
work together.

21

Name _____

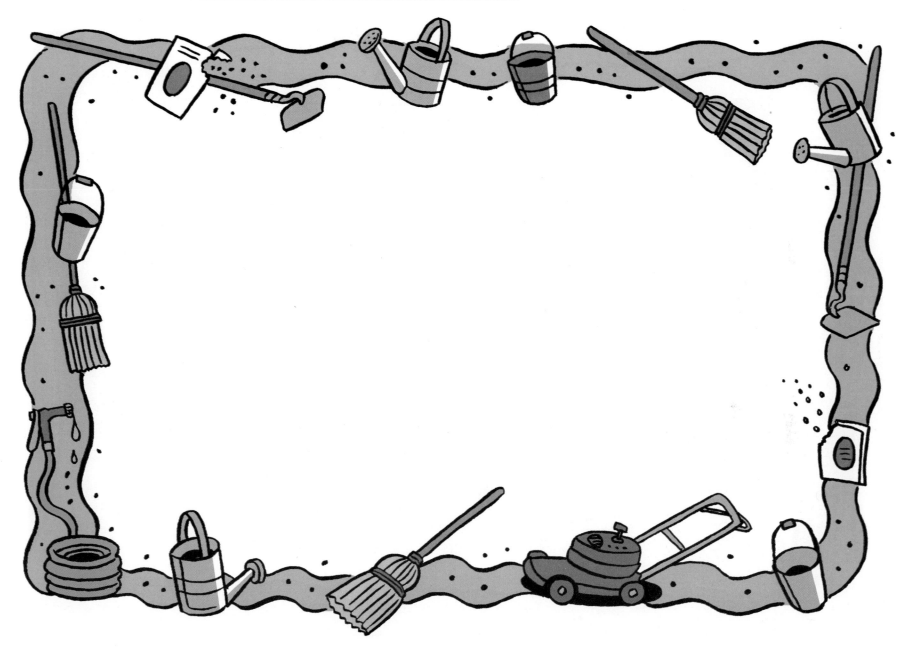

To the Teacher
Have children draw a picture of one way the little wolf in *Can I Help?* helps his
father. Then have them turn to page 24.

Lesson 6: Respond to Literature

Name _____

24

To the Teacher
Have children draw a picture of what happens at the end of the story.

Name _____

To the Teacher
Have children cut out the small pictures. Tell them to glue each cutout in an appropriate place on one of the large pictures. The outside is shown on the reverse side of this page.

Name _____

To the Teacher
Review with children what happens in the beginning, the middle, and the end of *Franklin's New Friend*. Have children write 1, 2, and 3 in the boxes to show the correct order. Then have partners retell the story.

Lesson 7: Respond to Literature

Name _____

28

To the Teacher
Have children talk about each picture. Then have them circle the appropriate child in a different color as you say each feeling word: *happy, sad, mad, proud, silly,* and *surprised.* For example, say: *Circle the sad child in blue.*

© Harcourt

Name _____

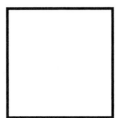

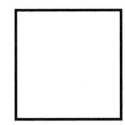

To the Teacher
Help children identify what is happening in each story panel. Then have them number the panels 1, 2, and 3 to show the correct story order of *Jazzbo and Googy*. Have partners retell the story.

29

© Harcourt

Name _____

To the Teacher
Help children identify each picture. Then have them draw a line from the animals on the left to the picture on the right that shows how the animals help people.

Name _____

5 [ ] nap.

4 [ ] nap.

3 [ ] nap.

2 [ ] nap.

✂

To the Teacher
Have children cut out the pictures of the animals. Then have them count the animals
in each picture and paste it in the sentence that matches that number. Then have
children turn to page 32.

31

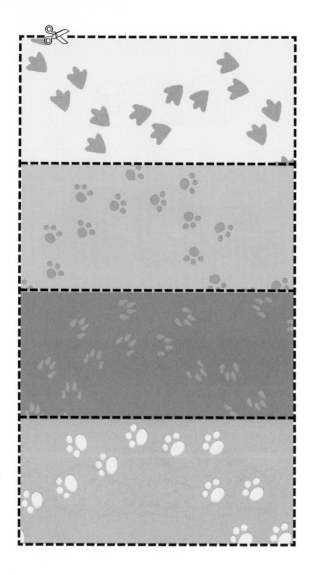

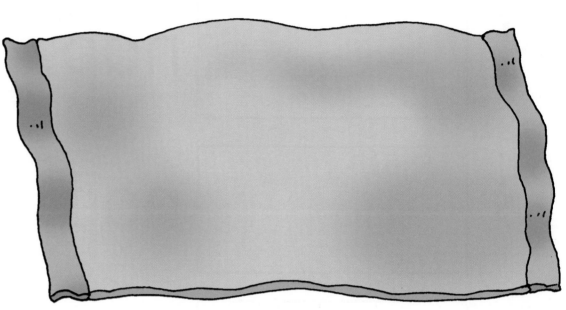

I nap.

To the Teacher
Have children draw a picture of themselves napping.

We go.

8

We Go

by Tim Pritchard   illustrated by Jane Chambers Wright

Harcourt

Bears go.

Raccoons go.

6

Squirrels go.

Rabbits go.

3

Unit 2: Take-Home Book

Deer go.

Skunks go.

Name _____

● ● ● ● ●

● ● ● ● ●

To the Teacher
Help children identify each picture. Then have them match the items for babies to
the items for older children.

37

Name _____

Lesson 11: Respond to Literature

38

To the Teacher
Review with children what happens in the story *Big Sarah's Little Boots*. Have children write 1, 2, or 3 in each box to show the beginning, middle, and end of the story.

Name _____

To the Teacher
Help children cut out the baby animals and glue them next to their mothers.
Then have children complete the activity on the reverse side of this page.

Lesson 12: Words of the Week

Name _____

To the Teacher
Have children draw their favorite baby animal.

Name _____

To the Teacher
Have children cut out the mother animals and ask them to glue them on the page to show how they help their babies. Then have children complete the activity on the reverse side of this page.

Lesson 12: Respond to Literature

Lesson 12: Respond to Literature

To the Teacher
Have children circle one baby animal at the top of the page. Then ask them to draw a picture of what that baby animal will look like when it grows up.

© Harcourt

Name_____

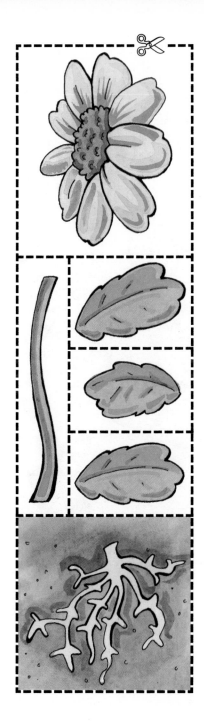

To the Teacher
Have children cut out the parts of the plant. Have them glue the parts in place to form a plant.

Lesson 13: Words of the Week

Lesson 13: Words of the Week

To the Teacher
Help children identify the part of each plant that is missing. Then have them draw the missing part to complete each plant.

Name _____

To the Teacher
Help children name the foods shown around the salad bowl. Then have them draw
and write about what they would include in a salad.

Lesson 13: Respond to Literature

Name _____

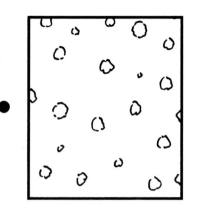

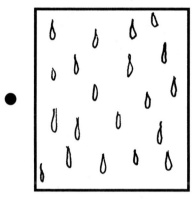

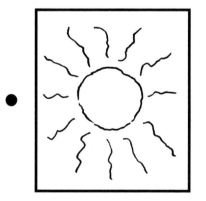

To the Teacher
Have children draw lines to match the scenes on the left to the pictures on the right. Then have them color the pictures.

To the Teacher

Help children cut out the story panels and use them to retell what happens in *Rain*. Ask them to rearrange the panels in order and tell the story to a partner. Then have children put together the puzzle on the reverse side.

47

Lesson 14: Respond to Literature

My mom has me.

8

The Dog Has Pups

by Jeffrey Allen

Harcourt

The dog has pups.

The fox has a pup.

6

The pig has piglets.

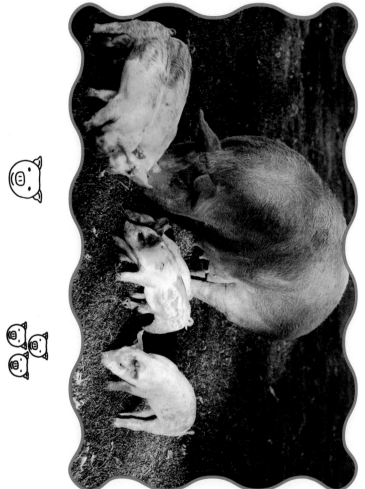

The goat has a kid.

3

Unit 3: Take-Home Book

The cat has a kitten.

The bear has cubs.

4

Unit 3: Take-Home Book

Name _____

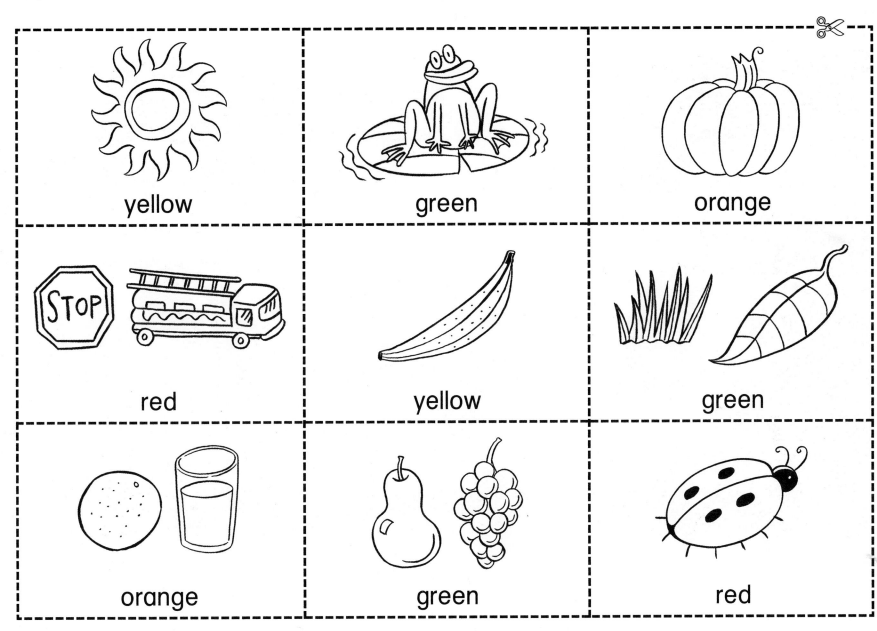

yellow	green	orange
red	yellow	green
orange	green	red

To the Teacher
Help children identify the pictures and have them fill in each box with the
appropriate color. Then have children cut out the cards and work with a partner
to sort them by color.

53

© Harcourt

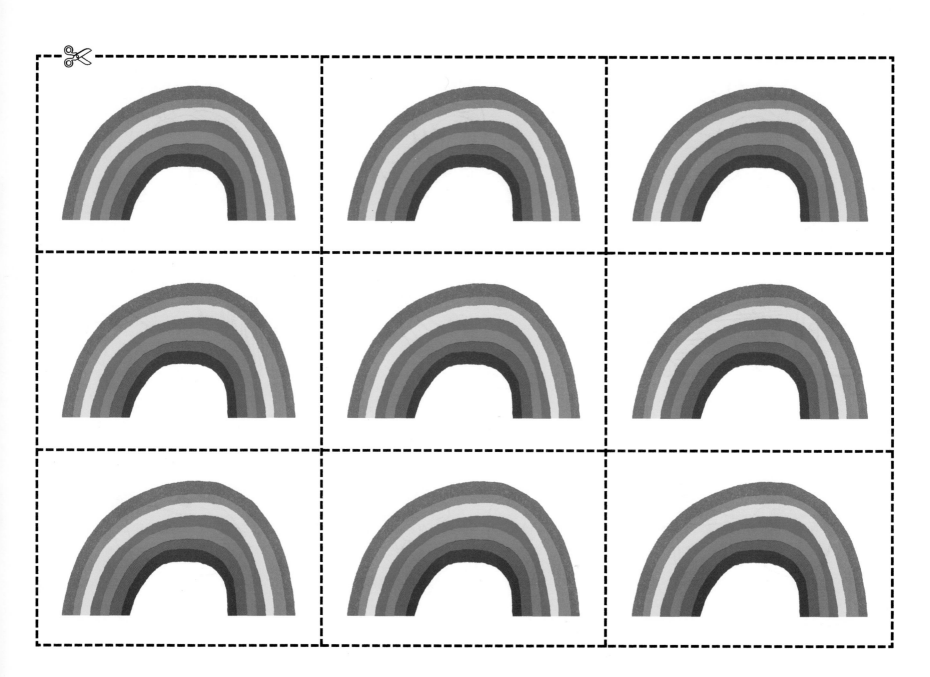

Name _____

To the Teacher
Have children cut out the puppets, tape them to craft sticks, and act out how the
crayons felt about each other at the beginning of the story. Then have them draw
faces, arms, and legs on the large crayons to show how they felt at the beginning.

55

Lesson 16: Respond to Literature

56

To the Teacher
Have children use the puppets to act out how the crayons felt about each other at the end of the story. Then have them draw faces, arms, and legs on the large crayons to show how they felt at the end.

Name _____

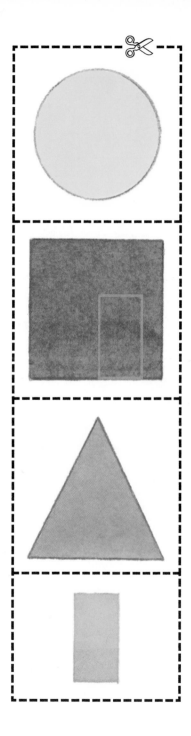

To the Teacher
Help children cut out the shapes. Then ask them to glue each shape where it belongs in the picture.

Lesson 17: Words of the Week

© Harcourt

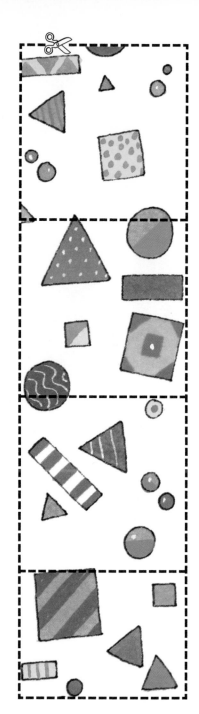

Lesson 17: Words of the Week

58

To the Teacher
Discuss with children what the dotted shape in each picture could be (window, sail, clock, and so on). Then have them trace each shape and add details to it.

© Harcourt

Name _____

To the Teacher
Help children identify each shape. Then ask them to draw something inside each
shape. Have them tell about their pictures.

59

Lesson 17: Respond to Literature

Name _____

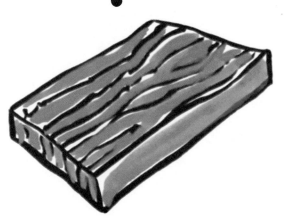

To the Teacher
Have children draw a line from each tool to the correct item.

© Harcourt

Name _____

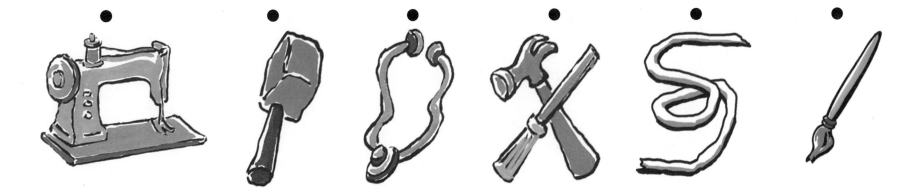

To the Teacher
Help children identify the pictures from the story *We Can Fix*. Then have them draw a line from each picture in the top row to the tool used to help fix it in the story.

Lesson 18: Respond to Literature

Name _____

© Harcourt

To the Teacher
Have children discuss what the bears are doing in each picture. Then have children circle the picture for each word (*jump, run, walk, dance, sing*) in a different color. For example, say: *Circle the picture of the bears singing in* **red.**

Name _____

To the Teacher
Review with children the three dances that Bear does in *Moondance.* Have children write 1, 2, or 3 in the boxes to show the order of his dances. Then have children complete the activity on the reverse side.

Lesson 19: Respond to Literature

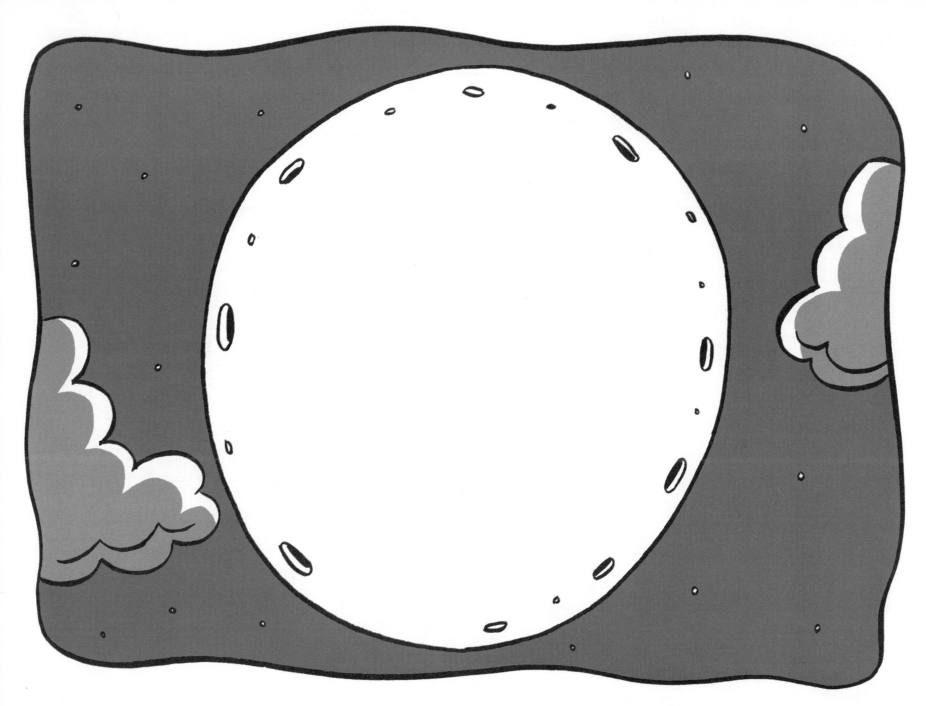

Lesson 19: Respond to Literature

64

To the Teacher
Have children draw a picture of Bear dancing in the moon.

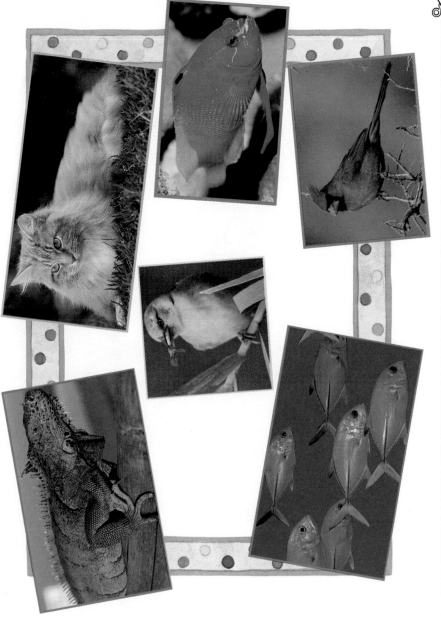

8

I Am

by Lisa Kindrey   Illustrated by Stephanie Peterson

Harcourt

___   ___

I am blue.

I am orange.

6

I am purple.

I am red.

3

© Harcourt

5

I am yellow.

I am green.

4

Name _____

To the Teacher
Have children circle the appropriate object in a different color as you say each of
the Words of the Week: *room, bed, chair, window,* and *lamp.* For example, say: *Circle the
bed in red.*

Lesson 21: Words of the Week

Name _____

Tonight

Tomorrow

To the Teacher
Help children identify the story event in each picture on the left. Then have them draw a line from each picture to *tonight* or *tomorrow* depending on when it happened or was going to happen in the story.

Lesson 21: Respond to Literature

© Harcourt

Name _____

To the Teacher
Have children cut out the pictures of the places and things. Help them identify
each picture and glue it in the appropriate place. Have partners discuss the
completed scene. Then have children circle each place or thing they see in their
own neighborhood on the reverse side.

71

Lesson 22: Words of the Week

Name _____

To the Teacher
Have children cut out the picture of the girl and glue it to a craft stick. Model how to move the puppet from picture to picture on both sides of the page as you say each sentence from *My Neighborhood*. Then have partners retell the story.

Lesson 22: Respond to Literature

© Harcourt

Name _____

To the Teacher
Have children cut out the pictures of the ways to get around and glue each one in the appropriate place on either side of this page.

Lesson 23: Words of the Week

Name _____

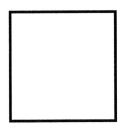

To the Teacher
Help children number the panels to retell the order of the events in the story.

Lesson 23: Respond to Literature

© Harcourt

Name _____

Police 1246

Teacher's Edition 1 2 A B

© Harcourt

Lesson 24: Words of the Week

78

To the Teacher
Help children identify the workers and the items. Ask them to draw a line from each worker to the item that he or she uses at work.

4

Name _____

PEOPLE WORK

1

To the Teacher
Help children cut out and fold the book. On pages 2 and 3, have children draw their favorite worker from *Communities* and the things he or she uses. Then ask them to write the first letter of the word for the worker's name.

Fold on dashed line.

Lesson 24: Respond to Literature

© Harcourt

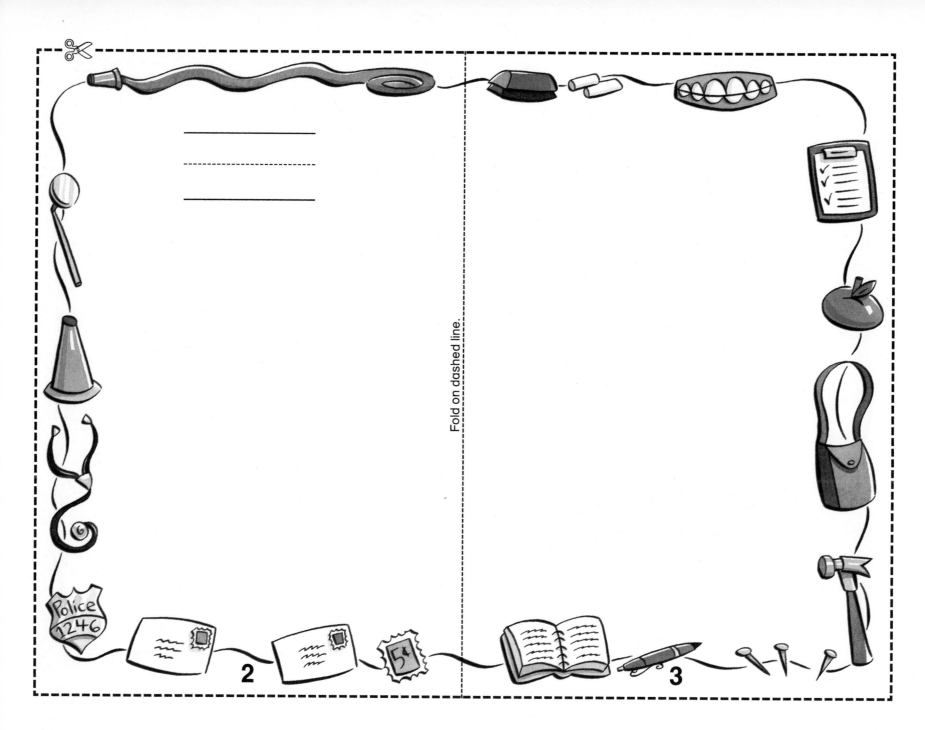

_____

- - - - - - - - - -

_____

Fold on dashed line.

2

3

© Harcourt

We like to go!

8

The Park

by Linley Stover   Illustrated by Paul Harvey

Harcourt

We go to the park.

We go on a train.

7

6

We go to the park.

We go on a bus.

3

We go to the park.

4

5

We go on a bike.

Name _____

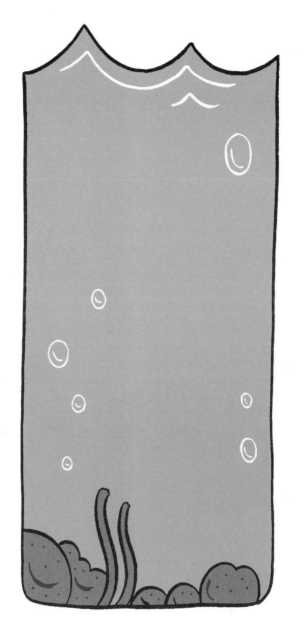

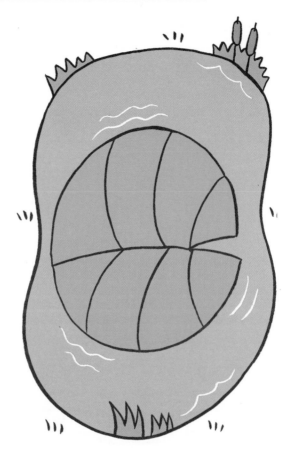

To the Teacher
Have children cut out the animals. Ask them to glue each animal to the correct
scene. Ask children to describe each animal and its surroundings. Then have them
draw a picture of one Word of the Week in the frame on the reverse side.

85

Lesson 26: Words of the Week

Name _____

To the Teacher
Help children cut out the story panels and use them to retell *Come Along, Daisy*.
Have children arrange the panels in story order and then tell the story to a partner.
Partners can then put together the pieces of the puzzle on the reverse side.

87

Lesson 26: Respond to Literature

Name _____

land

water

To the Teacher
Help children identify each picture as either land or water. Have them cut out and paste the pictures in the correct place. Then have children choose one Word of the Week and draw it in the frame on the reverse side.

89

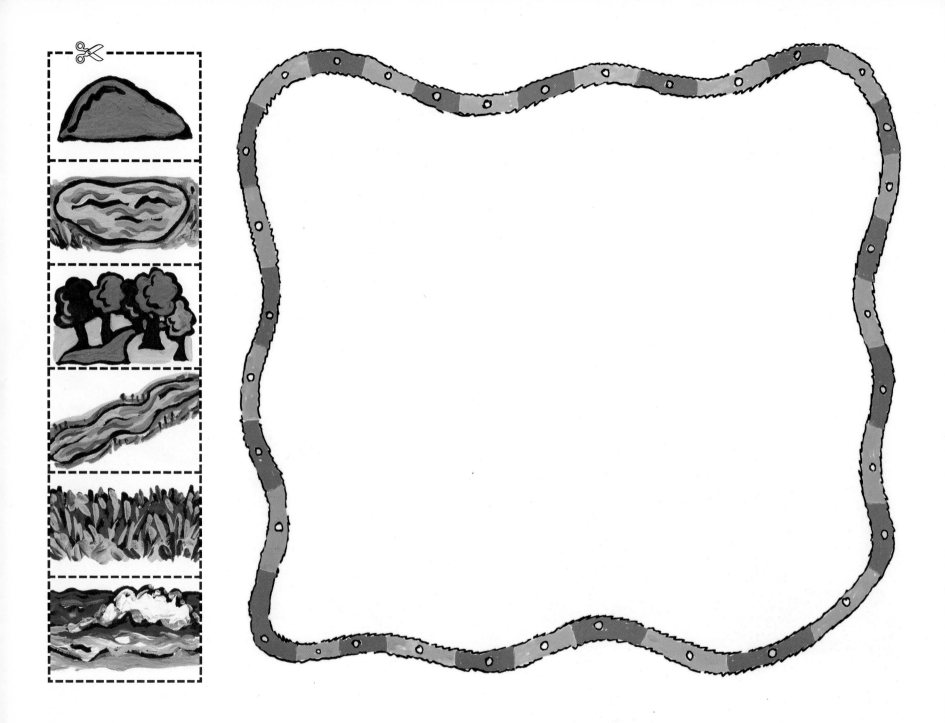

Name_____

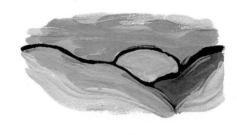

● ● ● ●

● ● ● ●

To the Teacher
Help children identify each picture at the top of the page and determine which
one belongs with each character. Tell them to draw a line from each item to the
appropriate character.

Lesson 27: Respond to Literature

Name _____

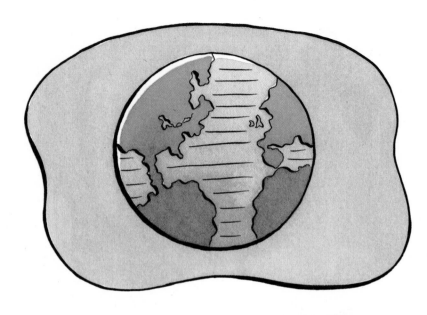

To the Teacher
Have children discuss with partners what is happening in each picture. Then read aloud the Words of the Week and have children circle each picture or part of the picture in a different color as you read each word: *Earth, save, clean, recycle, planet, care, litter, trashcan.* For example, say: *Circle the people who are cleaning in red.*

Name_____

●　　　　　　　●　　　　　　　●　　　　　　　●

●　　　　　　　●　　　　　　　●　　　　　　　●

To the Teacher
Help children identify each picture from I *Went to the Bay*. Ask them to match each
animal to where the boy saw it in the story.

Lesson 28: Respond to Literature

Name _____

To the Teacher
Have partners discuss the illustration. Then ask children to circle each star they see.

To the Teacher

Discuss what is happening in each picture. Have children cut out the pictures and place them in the order in which they appear in the story. Have partners use them to retell the story. Children can then put together the pieces of the puzzle on the reverse side.

95

Lesson 29: Respond to Literature

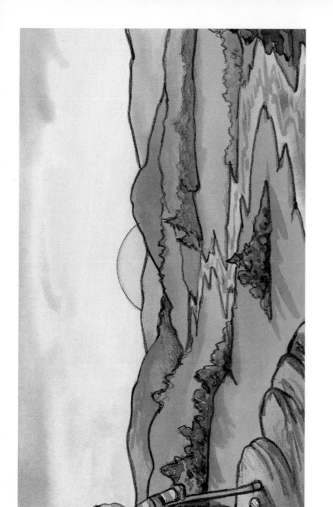

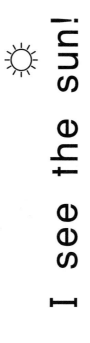

I see the sun!

8

© Harcourt

Our Earth

by Asa Spahn   illustrated by Roberta Collier-Morales

Harcourt

What do I see?

© Harcourt

I see a bear.

6

I see a rabbit.

I see a fox.

3

Unit 6: Take-Home Book

I see a deer.

I see a bird.

4

Word Bank

People Words

 baby	 boy	 children
 girl	 man	 student
 teacher	 team	 woman

Action Words

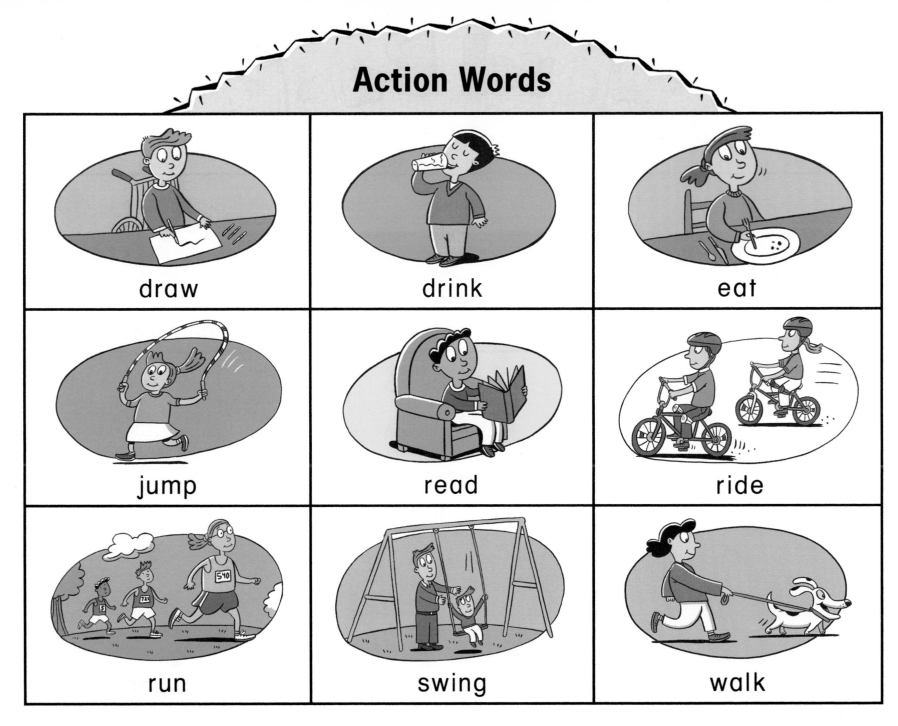

draw

drink

eat

jump

read

ride

run

swing

walk

Food Words

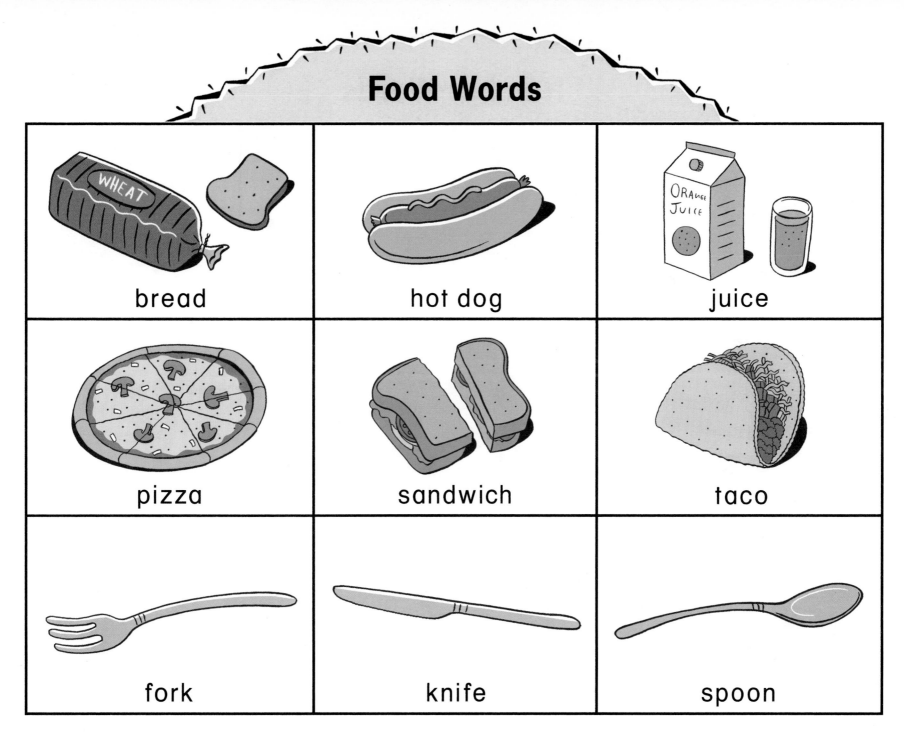

bread	hot dog	juice
pizza	sandwich	taco
fork	knife	spoon

Number Words

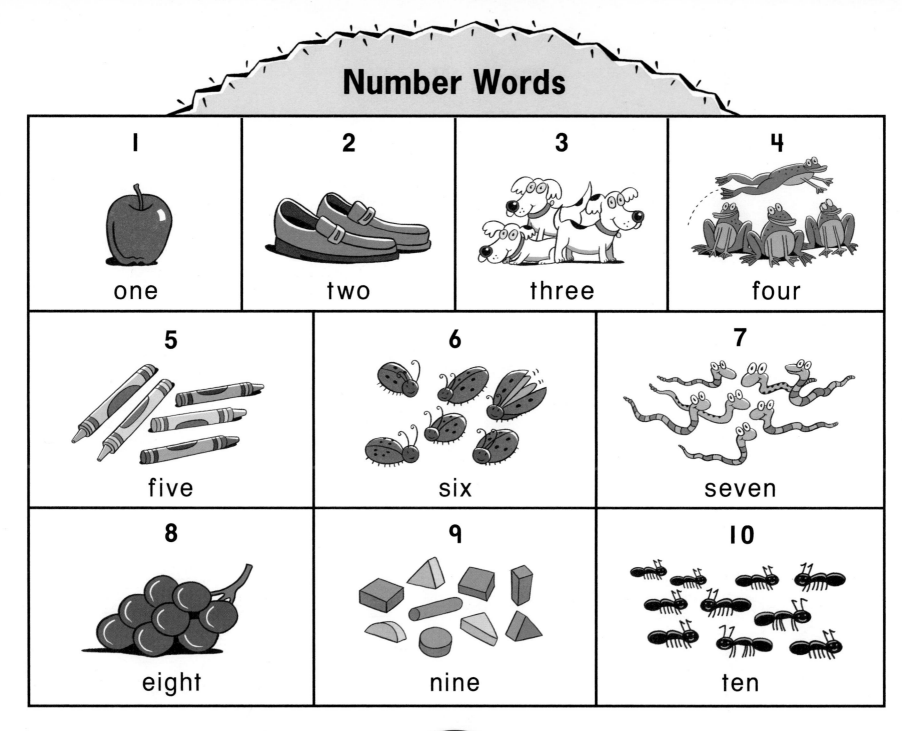

1 one	**2** two	**3** three	**4** four
5 five	**6** six	**7** seven	
8 eight	**9** nine	**10** ten	